EARTH BORERS

BY RYAN NAGELHOUT

Gareth Stevens
PUBLISHING

Please visit our website, www.garethstevens.com. For a free color catalog of all our high-quality books, call toll free 1-800-542-2595 or fax 1-877-542-2596.

Cataloging-in-Publication Data

Names: Nagelhout, Ryan.
Title: Earth borers / Ryan Nagelhout.
Description: New York : Gareth Stevens, 2017. | Series: Technology takes on nature | Includes index.
Identifiers: ISBN 9781482457834 (pbk.) | ISBN 9781482457858 (library bound) | ISBN 9781482457841 (6 pack)
Subjects: LCSH: Earthmoving machinery–Juvenile literature. | Excavating machinery–Juvenile literature.
Classification: LCC TA725.N34 2017 | DDC 621.8′65–dc23

First Edition

Published in 2017 by
Gareth Stevens Publishing
111 East 14th Street, Suite 349
New York, NY 10003

Copyright © 2017 Gareth Stevens Publishing

Designer: Sarah Liddell
Editor: Ryan Nagelhout

Photo credits: Cover, pp. 1, 5, 15, 27 Bloomberg/Contributor/Bloomberg/Getty Images; background texture used throughout Rodrigo Bellizzi/Shutterstock.com; p. 6 vewfinder/Shutterstock.com; p. 7 Gina Ferazzi/Contributor/Los Angeles Times/Getty Images; pp. 9, 17 VILevi/Shutterstock.com; p. 10 W.Rebel/Wikimedia Commons; p. 11 David McNew/Staff/Getty Images News/Getty Images; p. 13 Sean Nel/Shutterstock.com; p. 18 Fedor Selivanov/Shutterstock.com; p. 19 Wdwdbot/Wikimedia Commons; p. 20 EQRoy/Shutterstock.com; p. 21 (main) SSPL/Getty Images; p. 21 (inset) Gary Perkin/Shutterstock.com; pp. 23, 24, 25 Dennis Bratland/Wikimedia Commons; p. 29 Armita/Shutterstock.com.

Printed in China

CPSIA compliance information: Batch #CW17GS: For further information contact Gareth Stevens, New York, New York at 1-800-542-2595.

CONTENTS

Words in the glossary appear in **bold** type the first time they are used in the text.

SAVING BERTHA

In 2014, the largest tunnel-boring machine (TBM) in the world got stuck 60 feet (18 m) beneath Seattle, Washington. Nicknamed "Bertha," the machine was supposed to chew through rock and dirt more than 200 feet (61 m) below downtown Seattle. When finished, it would create a 1.7-mile (2.7 km) tunnel big enough for four lanes of highway on two levels.

Tunneling machines, also called boring machines, are just one of the many ways people use **technology** to take on nature. Let's find out how engineers got Bertha unstuck and how they use tunnel-boring machines to create amazing tunnels all over the world.

BIG BERTHA

Bertha is one huge machine. Its steel cutting head and machinery measures 326 feet (99.4 m) long and 57.5 feet (17.5 m) wide and weighs 7,000 tons (6,350 mt). Built in a launch pit 80 feet (24.4 m) deep, Bertha's cutting head has 260 "teeth" used to chew through rock and dirt.

BEFORE BERTHA, THE BIGGEST TBM EVER BUILT WAS BIG BECKY. IT WAS A 47.2-FOOT (14.4 M) BORING MACHINE USED TO BUILD A TUNNEL IN NIAGARA FALLS, ONTARIO.

Bertha has gotten stuck several times since it first started **excavating** under Seattle in 2012. That's one of the many issues that come with digging underground. A boring machine is a large piece of **equipment** that can break easily. Its cutting head has teeth that turn rock and dirt into fine bits that are then taken out through the tunnel created by the machine's path.

When a machine breaks, however, it can't move backward. That means if a tunnel-boring machine gets stuck, workers have to dig around it to fix its head.

WHY A TUNNEL?

The tunnel Bertha is digging will replace the Alaskan Way **Viaduct**, a raised highway that runs through downtown Seattle. In 2001, an **earthquake** shook Seattle and damaged the over-60-year-old viaduct. City leaders decided a tunnel should replace it because it would be safer and would rejoin the city and the waterfront, which the viaduct had separated.

ALASKAN WAY VIADUCT

GOING UNDER

Boring machines use a special system to dig through rock and dirt and create the support system needed to keep the tunnel open after it's made. Each TBM is first put in place underground, then works to move itself forward along a specific path. Its face, called a shield or cutterhead, is pushed into the dirt and rock by special **hydraulic** presses.

The entire cutterhead spins as it moves forward, and special plates on it also spin to chew up rock, dirt, and clay. As the cutterhead spins, dirt and rock are ground into smaller pieces and move through holes in the cutterhead.

DIFFERENT FACES

The type of shield a TBM uses depends on the kind of matter it's going to be digging through. London's Crossrail **expansion** project, for example, used six earth-pressure TBMs and one mix-shield TBM. Earth-pressure machines move easily through dry clay and rock, while mix-shield TBMs work better in waterlogged riverbeds and other wet areas.

As the cutterhead is pressed deeper into new earth, dirt and rock begin to collect behind the shield in a spinning area called the mixing chamber. A screw-shaped tool moves this dirt toward the back of the TBM as it spins. This tool drops the debris, or waste, onto a conveyor belt that carries the material back to the other end of the TBM. This material is dumped into trucks and other carriers and is removed from the tunnel.

Once the cutterhead has bored a large enough area, the tunnel must be supported by concrete so it doesn't **collapse**.

DIFFERENT DEBRIS

Mix-shield TBMs used in waterlogged conditions have a special system in place to cut and deal with debris. A liquid called bentonite is added to the bubble of air behind the cutterhead that keeps pressure on the cutting face. The bentonite helps the bubble and debris keep the cutterhead in place.

CONTROL ROOM

MIXING CHAMBER

CONVEYOR BELT

CUTTERHEAD

SOME TBMs, LIKE BERTHA, USE LIQUIDS TO HELP BREAK DOWN ROCK AND DEBRIS INTO A PASTE.

PROTECTING THE TUNNEL

After the TBM has drilled a certain distance, it stops. A special **erector** arm moves premade, curved concrete pieces into place to form a ring. These concrete pieces are made at a special factory and match the size of the TBM's cutting head. When one ring is finished, the erector arm starts work on another one.

The rings form a wall in the tunnel to prevent the tunnel from collapsing behind the TBM as it moves forward. The rings are positioned so that each ring's joints never line up with the joints on either side of it. This prevents weak points in the wall.

MOVING ON

To keep them in place, these large concrete pieces are first glued together. Then, screws connect the pieces to make the tunnel stronger. Once a full ring of concrete pieces Is put in place, special jacks push the entire TBM further along through the new tunnel section.

THE TUNNEL LEFT BEHIND BY A TBM BECOMES A CONSTRUCTION SITE, AND DIRT IS CARRIED OUT AND SUPPLIES ARE CARRIED IN TO HELP THE TBM DIG FURTHER.

13

LAUNCHING BERTHA

To get Bertha underground, workers needed to dig it a pit. Called a launch pit, the space was about 80 feet (24 m) wide, 80 feet (24 m) deep, and 400 feet (122 m) long. Workers drilled posts, called piles, deep into the ground around the outside of Bertha's launch pit. The machine was put in place by a large crane.

When Bertha is hard at work under Seattle, it moves an average of 35 feet (10.7 m) per day. But boring-machine projects are often delayed by many different problems. There are always surprises when digging.

SMALL BORERS

Smaller boring machines are used for similar tunneling projects. These Small Boring Units usually have cutting heads 2 to 6 feet (0.6 to 1.8 m) in diameter and work the same way as full-size boring machines. They often build tunnels for cables, gas lines, and other small projects that dig under buildings, parks, or streets.

BIG TUNNEL PROJECTS NEED CAREFUL PLANNING SO TUNNELS AVOID SEWERS, POWER LINES, AND ANYTHING ELSE ALREADY BURIED UNDERGROUND.

BIG BECKY LAUNCH PIT

15

WATCHING CLOSELY

Once underway, TBM projects are monitored, or watched, closely. Behind the cutting head, workers in the control room check the cutterhead's power and speed using special sensing tools. They make sure hard rock or unexpected objects don't jam the machine. The workers in the control room also make sure the head doesn't drill too quickly, which could cause major problems such as **cave-ins**.

Other conditions around a tunneling project also need to be watched carefully. In Seattle, more than 200 buildings above or near the tunneling project are monitored to make sure they aren't moving as the tunnel is excavated.

TRACKING BERTHA

A $20 million program was put in place to make sure Bertha doesn't hurt the buildings and people above ground during tunneling. More than 900 **survey** points along its path use tools to check for movements in the soil and other changes that could mean buildings are shifting or supports are getting weaker.

TBMs CAN'T DO EVERYTHING ON A BIG DIG. CONSTRUCTION WORKERS ARE ALWAYS HELPING TO GET TBMs AND THE DIG SITE READY.

17

UNDER THE ALPS

The longest railroad tunnel in the world opened in
Switzerland in 2016. The Gotthard Base Tunnel stretches 35.4 miles
(57 km) under one of the tallest mountain ranges in the world—the
Alps. High-speed trains bring people and goods back and forth
through a tunnel that's up to 1.4 miles (2.3 km) below the mountains'
tall peaks.

Four TBMs worked to drill the two-layered tunnel route for
17 years. Engineers cut through 73 different kinds of rock and
excavated more than 31 tons (28 mt) of material to build the tunnel.
Some of that rock even made its way
into the concrete used
to support
the tunnel.

BELOW, NOT OVER

Before the Gotthard Base Tunnel, more than 1 million trucks a year carried goods between northern and southern Europe on roads through the mountains. It cost more than $12 billion to finish the project, but businesses say it will save millions per year in shipping costs.

THE CHUNNEL

One of the most famous tunnels in the world is a 31.4-mile (50.5 km) stretch that lets people travel between England and France by going underneath the English Channel. Digging started on both sides of the channel in 1988, with 11 TBMs digging down and across below the channel.

When the two tunnels met near the middle on December 1, 1990, a French worker and an English worker shook hands through a hole connecting the two tunnel ends. The Channel Tunnel, also called the "Chunnel," officially opened in 1994. At its lowest point, the tunnel dips 246 feet (75 m) below the waterway.

TRAIN THAT TRAVELS THROUGH THE CHUNNEL

A BORING MACHINE FROM THE ENGLISH SIDE STILL SITS BURIED UNDER THE CHANNEL TODAY. IN 2004, ONE OF THE MACHINES WAS EVEN SOLD ONLINE!

FRENCH CHUNNEL CUTTERHEAD

NEW LANDS

Soil and rock taken out of the Chunnel on the English side were added to an area called Shakespeare Cliff near Dover. The 90-acre (36 ha) spot is called Samphire Hoe. On the French side of the project, the dirt was used to create a large hill.

DIGGING INTO TROUBLE

The Chunnel's TBMs worked with few problems, but TBMs that do get damaged and stuck often see the same problems. Uneven soil, like the soil Bertha dug through in Seattle, can have unexpected surprises such as metal and hard material that breaks spinning cutterheads or gets them stuck.

Four months into the project, Bertha overheated and shut down. A shaft 83 feet (25 m) wide was dug down to reach the TBM. A special crane was then built to lift pieces of the cutterhead out of the tunnel to repair them.

MEGAPROJECTS

Large digging projects that cost more than $1 billion are often called "megaprojects." People who study these large projects often say they all have the same problems: they cost more than people think they will and take much longer. Or as one professor studying them said, "They're over budget, over time, over and over again."

BERTHA'S RESCUE SITE

23

Digging a shaft in Seattle's waterlogged soil created big problems when engineers rescued Bertha. Water filling the shaft needed to be pumped out by engineers as they worked. People believe this pumping caused the area around Bertha to sink, often an inch (2.54 cm) or more. People living in nearby buildings complained of cracking walls and moving building foundations.

Bertha started working again on December 22, 2015, but stopped again in January 2016 when a **sinkhole** opened near the project. Digging started again soon after, but many people, including Washington's governor, worry the project could put people at risk in the future.

END DIGGING

BIG BERTHA

BEGIN DIGGING

LONG DELAYS

Bertha's work was supposed to finish in 2015, but many delays have pushed its end date back. Project engineers say boring will finish sometime in 2017. As of late 2016, Bertha was in Zone 6 of 10. Much of the path Bertha will take goes under large buildings, which would make rescue hard if more trouble strikes.

SCRAP OR BURY?

Engineers aren't sure what will happen to Bertha after it's done digging under Seattle. Each TBM costs millions of dollars to build, but removing it from the tunnel after it's finished digging can cost millions more. These massive machines are rarely used for a second project. Instead, they're sometimes taken apart and sold for scrap.

Some are actually left underground when they finish digging. A TBM named Seli that cost between $6 million and $8 million was used to make a new subway tunnel underneath New York City. The drill, weighing 200 tons (181 mt) and measuring 22.5 feet (6.9 m) wide, was buried in 2011 and still sits under the city today!

STUCK UNDERGROUND

Dragados, the same company working on Seattle's tunneling project, decided selling Seli for scrap would actually cost them more money than they'd make. Seli would need to be taken apart and hauled to the other end of the tunnel. Dragados decided that would cost too much in construction delays and pay for workers.

THESE WORKERS ARE HELPING BUILD TUNNELS UNDER GRAND CENTRAL TERMINAL IN NEW YORK CITY. WORKERS WHO BUILD UNDERGROUND ARE CALLED SANDHOGS!

27

PUSHING THROUGH

Despite their many issues, tunnel-boring machines are important tools used to create modern marvels. And though they often get stuck or break down and need creative fixes to their problems, the tools do the hard work of digging safely underground.

Projects like London's Crossrail train network and the Chunnel underneath the English Channel saw few construction problems. Switzerland's massive tunnel underneath the Alps was another major engineering project that likely was not possible without the use of TBMs. As engineers work more with these giant grinding machines and find ways to fix the problems they encounter, they hope future projects will go more smoothly.

THE NEED TO FINISH

Once a TBM project is started, it's very hard to stop. The cost of TBMs and the project itself are often too much to abandon. Seattle is committed to letting Bertha finish the project no matter what issues they have during digging. "There's no turning back," said Tim Burgess, president of the Seattle City Council in 2014.

AMERICA'S LONGEST TUNNELS

ANTON ANDERSON MEMORIAL TUNNEL
ALASKA, OPENED 2000
13,727 FT (4,184 M) LONG

TED WILLIAMS/I90 EXTENSION TUNNEL
MASSACHUSETTS, OPENED 2003
13,780 FT (4,200 M) LONG

BROOKLYN BATTERY TUNNEL
NEW YORK, OPENED 1950
9,117 FT (2,779 M) LONG

LYNDON B. JOHNSON TUNNEL
TEXAS, OPENED 2016
9,843 FT (3,000 M) LONG

29

GLOSSARY

cave-in: a place where earth or rock has fallen in underground

collapse: to fall or sink quickly

earthquake: a shaking of a portion of Earth's crust

equipment: the tools needed to do a task

erector: a machine for putting together or constructing

excavate: to dig out and remove

expansion: the act or process of making bigger

hydraulic: operated by means of the pressure produced when a liquid is forced through a small opening or tube

sinkhole: a hollow place underground that suddenly collapses to form an open hole

survey: to look over closely

technology: a tool used in the science of solving problems

viaduct: a bridge

FOR MORE INFORMATION

BOOKS

Farndon, John. *Stickmen's Guide to Gigantic Machines*. Minneapolis, MN: Hungry Tomato, 2016.

Parker, Steve. *Giant Machines*. Broomall, PA: Mason Crest Publishers, 2011.

Stefoff, Rebecca. *Building Tunnels*. New York, NY: Cavendish Square Publishing, 2016.

WEBSITES

How the Channel Tunnel Was Built
www.eurotunnel.com/uk/build/
Learn more about how the tunnel between the UK and France was built under the English Channel!

Tracking Bertha
wsdot.wa.gov/Projects/Viaduct/About/FollowBertha
Follow Bertha as the machine digs underneath Seattle.

INDEX